POPULAR
Quilling

POPULAR
Quilling

HELEN WALTER

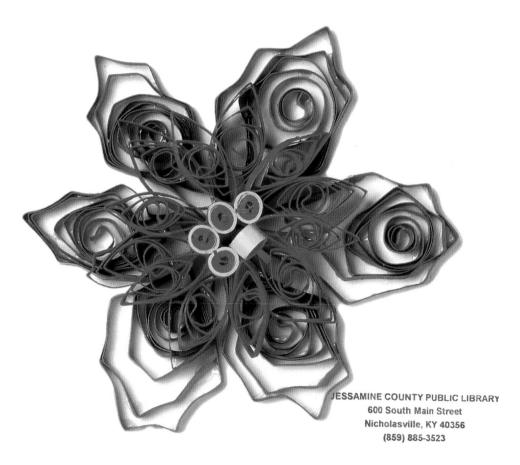

SALLYMILNER
PUBLISHING

First published in 2004 by
Sally Milner Publishing Pty Ltd
PO Box 2104
Bowral NSW 2576
AUSTRALIA

© Helen Walter 2004

Design: Anna Warren, Warren Ventures
Editing: Anne Savage
Photography: Tim Connolly

Printed in China

National Library of Australia Cataloguing-in-Publication data:

Walter, Helen.
    Popular quilling.

    ISBN 1 86351 338 8.

    1. Paper quillwork. 2. Paper quillwork - Patterns.
    I. Title. (Series : Milner craft series).

745.54
Walt

Disclaimer
The information in this instruction book is presented in good faith. However, no warranty is given, nor results
guaranteed, nor is freedom from any patent to be inferred. Since we have no control over the use of information
contained in this book, the publisher and the author disclaim liability for untoward results.

10 9 8 7 6 5 4 3 2 1

Contents

Introduction

In this, my third book of quilling designs, I have branched out a little and introduced some designs that are not floral. This has been a challenge and when all is said and done I have to admit that I find flowers are still the most rewarding things to quill. Their natural shapes just transpose into this medium with ease. I had thought I would have run out of flowers by now, but it seems there are still quite a few remaining that I haven't tried to quill, even in this book.

I hope that quillers worldwide will find something in here that will appeal to them and inspire them to create their own designs. Remember that your shapes don't have to be perfect and identical—after all, nature herself has variations in colour and size of flowers, birds and animals. Enjoy!

Notes

Unless specified otherwise, all designs use 3 mm (⅛ in) quilling papers.

A standard size blank card, 11 x 15 cm (6 in) (4½ x 6 in), has been used to display all the quilled designs. I have used cream or white cards for nearly all the designs but there are some great earthy colours as well as some delicate pastel shades now available that will add a distinctly unique look to your card.

Quilled cards can be posted! Just cut a piece of bubble-wrap to fit over your design before placing it in the envelope. Make sure you keep the quilled part away from where the stamp will go. Some of the designs may need to be packaged in a small box as they will be too thick to fit into an envelope without being damaged.

Basic quilling equipment

Quilling is a simple, portable and affordable craft. Expensive equipment is not required, and you don't need a lot of room to work in. You will need the following equipment to make any of the designs shown in this book.

Quilling papers of varying widths
The most commonly used are 3 mm (⅛ in), 4 mm (5⁄16), 6 mm (¼ in) and 10 mm (⅜ in). They are available from most craft suppliers.

Slotted quilling tool
This tool is used for coiling the strips of quilling paper. If you are handy it is a simple task to make your own tool from a piece of wooden dowelling 10 cm (4 in) long, and a tapestry needle. Insert the pointed end of the needle firmly into one end of the dowel, then nip off the very end of the eye with a pair of pliers to create the slot. To purchase a ready-made tool ask your local craft supplier.

Tweezers
These are available from the supermarket or pharmacy. Flat-jawed tweezers are the best. They are used to hold the quilled shape while applying glue, and to place the glued shapes into position on the card.

Scissors
I find small, pointed scissors are the most useful.

Ruler or tape measure

Used to measure the lengths of quilling paper specified.

Toothpicks

These are available at supermarkets. Use them to apply the glue to the quilled shape.

White PVA glue

Several brands are available from craft shops, hardware stores and newsagents. A clear-drying type is a must. Only a small amount is needed.

Blank cards

White or coloured blank cards can be purchased from craft shops or printers' suppliers.

Fringing tool

Several of the designs in this book include fringed parts and a fringing tool will make the job much easier. Cutting even slits with scissors becomes very tedious!

Basic quilling techniques and shapes

Measure the length of quilling paper required, then tear or cut it to length. Slide one end of the paper into the slot of the quilling tool and wind it to make a coil. For a tight coil apply glue to the end while still on the tool. For a loose coil take it off the tool and put it on the work surface in front of you. Allow the coil to loosen before glueing the end. Use your fingers to squeeze the loose coils to the required shape. Hold the quilled shape or strip with the tweezers while you apply glue with the toothpick, then place the shape on the card in the required position.

Tight coil

Wind a strip into a coil, then glue the end of the strip while still on the tool without allowing it to unwind.

Loose coil

Wind a tight coil and take it off the tool, allowing it to loosen before glueing the end of the strip.

Teardrop

Make a loose coil and pinch one side to a point to resemble a teardrop shape.

Bent teardrop

Make a teardrop shape and bend the pinched end.

Eye

Make a loose coil and pinch the opposite sides evenly to resemble an eye.

Leaf

Make a loose coil and pinch into an eye shape. Then bend the pinched ends in opposite directions.

Triangle

Make a loose coil and pinch three corners to make a triangle shape.

Arrow

Make a loose coil and pinch to a triangle shape. Pinch two corners firmly to form an arrow shape.

Crescent

Make a loose coil and pinch two points. Bend to make a crescent moon.

Half moon

Make a loose coil and pinch two points to make one flat side and one rounded side.

Beehive

Roll a tight coil into a cone shape and glue the end before taking it off the tool.

Birdfoot

Make a loose coil and shape into a triangle. Bend all three points in the same direction and squeeze firmly.

Star

Roll a loose coil and pinch five points evenly around it to make a star shape.

Diamond

Make an eye and then push fingers together to make a diamond shape.

Holly

Make a loose coil. Pinch it all the way around until it looks like a holly leaf.

How to make rose flowers

Step 1: Take the 20 cm (8 in) strip of 10 mm (⅜ in) wide paper and place one end into the slot of the quilling tool.

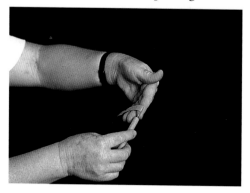

Step 2: Roll three turns on the tool and put on a spot of glue to hold in place.

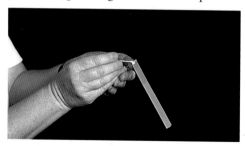

Step 3: Fold the paper towards you at a right angle and roll, allowing the top edge to flare out but keeping the bottom edge firmly against the tool.

Step 4: Add a spot of glue to hold, and continue to fold and roll the paper, glueing at every turn until you reach the end of the paper strip.

Step 5: Fold the end of the strip under the rose and glue to hold in place. Leave the rose on the tool until it can be removed without unravelling. You may need to add a few more dabs of glue in strategic places! Your rose is complete.

How to make fringed flowers

Step 1: Measure and cut the lengths of plain and fringed quilling papers.

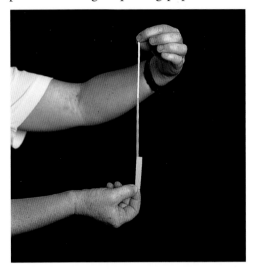

Step 2: Glue the pieces end to end in the prescribed order to make a long strip of quilling paper.

Step 3: Allow the glue to dry for a few moments, then insert the plain end into the slot of the quilling tool and commence to roll into a tight coil. Glue end while still on the tool.

Step 4: Remove from tool and gently spread fringes with your fingertips. Your fringed flower is complete!

Australia's outback

Mention the Australian outback and the first things that spring to mind are kangaroos, Uluru and red dust. But there is so much more than this—the vast red sandy tracts of desert, the sudden blooming of wildflowers after good rains, the clear starry skies and the sense of quietness and solitude. The outback is a special place that unfortunately is becoming so much more accessible that the very aspects that make it so appealing are now becoming endangered by too many visitors.

SANDALWOOD
Santalum spicatum

The Sandalwood is a medium sized shrubby tree bearing quantities of brown fruit, appealing to birds, of a similar size to those of its close relative, the edible Quandong (S. acuminatum). The Sandalwood is semi-parasitic, relying in large part on the roots systems of other trees for nutrition and is thus unsuitable for cultivation. It is found mainly in inland Western Australia and South Australia. Its main claim to fame is its perfumed wood, which is widely sought after in Asia for the production of incense.

Part	Quantity	Length	Shape	Colour
Fruit	6	15 cm (6 in)	loose coil	mid-brown
	1	8 cm (3 in)	loose coil	mid-brown
Leaves	30	8 cm (3 in)	eye	sage green
Stems	1	12 cm ($4^3/_4$ in)	strip	brown
	1	9 cm ($3^1/_2$ in)	strip	brown
	1	6 cm ($2^1/_4$ in)	strip	brown
	3	4 cm ($1^1/_2$ in)	strip	brown
	2	3.5 cm ($1^3/_8$ in)	strip	brown
	3	2 cm ($^3/_4$ in)	strip	brown

Arrangement

Bend all of the stems into Z shapes, then straighten slightly to fit onto your card. Position the three longest stems and glue down. Add remaining stems. Take the loose coils for the fruit and ever so slightly pinch one side to a point, keeping the rest of the shape round. Position the fruit and leaves as desired and glue into place.

WINDMILL

The windmill is an icon of the Australian outback. The silhouette of a windmill, its blades revolving slowly against a vivid orange sunset, is a popular image for photographers and travel brochures. Windmills in outback Australia are chiefly used for pumping water from underground bores and wells to supply domestic stock and remote homesteads and communities. Windmills hold a fascination for many people; the technical term for the study of windmills is 'molinology'.

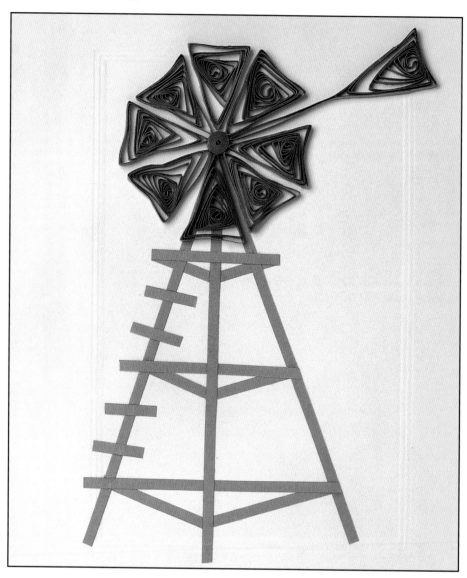

Part	Quantity	Length	Shape	Colour
Fan blades	8	40 cm (16 in)	triangle	grey
Fan centre	1	20 cm (8 in)	tight coil	grey
Tail	1	45 cm (18 in)	triangle	grey
	1	10 cm (4 in)	strip	grey
Tower legs	3	11 cm (4¼ in)	strip	grey
Crossbars	9	assorted	strip	grey
Steps	4	1.5 cm (½ in)	strip	grey

Construct the tower first. The whole of the tower is made with the quilling paper flat rather then on edge. Take the three 11 cm (4¼ in) strips and join them together at one end, fanning them out to make a tall triangular tower. Add the crosspieces and then the steps as illustrated. It is easier to make the crosspieces longer than required and to trim them with scissors once they are glued.

To make the tail, take the 10 cm (4 in) strip and fold it in half, creasing firmly. Then insert the 45 cm (18 in) triangle into the open end and glue them together.

Arrangement

Position the completed tower onto your card and glue down. Place the fan centre on the top point of the tower and glue. Arrange the fan blades around the centre so each has one point touching the centre. Position the tail between two of the fan blades so that the bar end touches the fan centre. When satisfied with your arrangement, glue into place.

To make the design brighter, make the tail and centre from different coloured papers, or make the fan blades different colours.

EMU

Dromaius novaehollandiae

The emu is a large flightless bird that can run at speeds of over 40 kilometres (25 miles) per hour and, in the words of the Australian singer/songwriter John Williamson, 'He can't fly but I'm tellin' you, he can run the pants off a kangaroo!' Emus are to be found over most of mainland Australia and during times of drought become quite a nuisance to wheat farmers by moving onto their crops in large numbers. The emu is depicted on the Australian coat-of-arms along with that other well-known Australian icon, the kangaroo.

Part	Quantity	Length	Shape	Colour
Head	1	12 cm (4³⁄₄ in)	teardrop	brown
Eye	1	2 cm (³⁄₄ in)	tight coil	lemon
Neck	7	8 cm (3 in)	tight coil	brown
Body	1	60 cm (24 in)	half moon	brown
Legs	2	5 cm (2 in)	strip	brown
Feet	2	10 cm (4 in)	birdfoot	brown
Spinifex grass	5	2 cm (³⁄₄ in)	strip	green

Arrangement

Glue the body onto the card first, followed by the neck and head angling downwards. Insert the eye. Fold the two 5 cm (2 in) strips for the legs in half, creasing them firmly, and then open them out to the desired angle before glueing them on under the centre of the body. Add the feet.

Arrange the green strips so they look like a tussock of grass and glue them onto the card below the emu's head so it looks as if he is searching for something to eat.

EMU CHICKS

Emu chicks are incubated and raised by the male emu. The female lays the eggs in the nest and then clears out, leaving the childcare up to Dad. After sitting on the eggs for eight weeks, during which time he can lose 4–8 kilograms (2–4 pounds) of weight, the male continues to care for the chicks for up to eighteen months. Emu eggs are large, with thick, textured shells of a dark greeny blue colour, with a lighter creamy white layer beneath. They are highly sought after for carving. The contents of the egg are 'blown' (removed through a small hole drilled in one end) and the artist incises the most exquisite pictures on the outside.

Part	Quantity	Length	Shape	Colour
Chick 1				
Body	1	20 cm (8 in)	strip	black
	1	18 cm (3 in)	strip	white
Head	1	6 cm (2¼ in)	strip	black
	1	4 cm (1½ in)	strip	white
Neck	3	5 cm (2 in)	strip	black
	3	4 cm (1½ in)	strip	white
Eye	1	2 cm (¾ in)	tight coil	lemon
Legs	2	1.5 cm (½ in)	strip	black
Feet	2	6 cm (2¼ in)	birdfoot	black
Chicks 2 and 3 are the same.				
Grass	4	1 cm (⅜ in)	strip	green

To make the body and head, roll the black and white strips together to make a loose coil, making sure that the black is on the outside. After glueing, squeeze the body to an eye shape, and the head to a teardrop shape.

To make the neck, roll the black and white strips together to make three tight coils, making sure that the black is on the outside. Glue while still on the quilling tool.

To make the legs, fold each strip in half and crease firmly, then bend them out until they are at the desired angle.

Arrangement

Starting with the body of the first chick, place it in the required position on the card. Add the neck and head. Insert the eye. Add the legs and feet. Do the same for the other chicks. When you are satisfied with your arrangement, glue them onto the card. Arrange the four short green strips to look like a grass tussock, and glue them on edge. If you want more grass, just add a few more green strips.

RED KANGAROO
Macropus rufus

Many visitors from overseas expect to see kangaroos as they emerge from the air-conditioned buildings at the international airports. Sadly, they are doomed to disappointment! Kangaroos prefer the country life, though many are not averse to lingering along the sides of the major highways! The kangaroo features in the Australian coat-of-arms and also makes an appearance on the 50 cent and $1 coins.

Part	Quantity	Length	Shape	Colour
Head	1	15 cm (6 in)	teardrop	brown
Ears	2	3 cm (1⅛ in)	strip	brown
	2	3 cm (1⅛ in)	strip	tan
Eyes	2	3 cm (1⅛ in)	tight coil	black
Arms	2	20 cm (8 in)	leaf	brown
Chest	1	25 cm (10 in)	diamond	tan
Left leg	1	30 cm (12 in)	eye	brown
		30 cm (12 in)	crescent	brown
Tail	1	30 cm (12 in)	crescent	brown
Feet	2	15 cm (6 in)	crescent	brown

To make the ears, glue a 3 cm (1⅛ in) tan strip to a 3 cm (1⅛ in) brown strip. Starting from the tan end, roll into a loose coil and glue the end. When dry squeeze it into a teardrop shape.

Arrangement

Assemble all the pieces into the finished design on the card and then glue each piece in place. To make a grey kangaroo, just change colours.

GHOST GUM
Eucalyptus papuana

Approximately 450 species of eucalypt are recognised by botanists; virtually all of them occur naturally only in Australia. A number of species have been very successfully introduced overseas, notably in California and countries around the Mediterranean. The Ghost Gums of the outback have smooth white powdery trunks with contrasting green drooping foliage. They should not be confused with the grey-trunked River Red Gum. The Ghost Gum has achieved international recognition through the watercolour paintings of the Australian artist Albert Namatjira, and tourists regularly visit a particular group of trees near Alice Springs which were the models for his paintings.

Part	Quantity	Length	Shape	Colour
Leaves	12	30 cm (12 in)	leaf	sage green
	3	30 cm (12 in)	crescent	sage green
Flowers	4	5 cm (2 in)	fringed 10 mm ($3/8$ in) strip	cream
	4	5 cm (2 in)	strip	cream
	4	10 cm (4 in)	beehive	sage green
Gum nuts	5	10 cm (4 in)	beehive	dark brown
	13	10 cm (4 in)	beehive	sage green
	13	9 cm ($3\frac{1}{2}$ in)	beehive	fawn
Stems	2	13 cm ($1\frac{1}{8}$ in)	strip	fawn
	1	5 cm (2 in)	strip	fawn
	1	5 cm (2 in)	strip	dark brown

To make the gum nuts, glue the 9 cm (3½ in) fawn beehives into the 10 cm (4 in) sage beehives to create a capsule.

To make the flowers, join together the 5 cm (2 in) cream strip and the 5 cm (2 in) fringed 10 mm (⅜ in) cream strip. Starting from the plain end, roll into a tight coil. Insert into a 10 cm (4 in) sage beehive before spreading the fringes out gently with your fingers.

Arrangement

Arrange the stems on the card so they are hanging down from the top. Add the leaves, gum nuts and flowers randomly until you are satisfied with the arrangement. Glue everything firmly to the card.

YATE

Eucalyptus cornuta

The buds of the Yate are the things that really give this tree character. They look like a witch's fingers! The Yate was the first of the Western Australian eucalypts to be named, in 1799. The first specimen was collected in 1792. The wood of the Yate is very strong and was often in the early days used to make wheels and shafts. It grows naturally in the south-west of Western Australia. The Yate is a fast-growing tree, ideal for windbreaks. It flowers during January and February.

Part	Quantity	Length	Shape	Colour
Stems	1	13 cm (5 in)	strip	light brown
	2	6 cm (2 $\frac{1}{4}$ in)	strip	light brown
	3	5 mm ($\frac{5}{16}$ in)	strip	light brown
Leaves	2	30 cm (12 in)	bent teardrop	sage green
	3	60 cm (24 in)	bent teardrop	sage green
Flowerets	15	5 cm (2 in)	fringed	lemon
			10 mm ($\frac{3}{8}$ in) tight coil	
	15	8 cm (3 in)	beehive	sage green
Buds	4	12 cm (4 $\frac{3}{4}$ in)	10 mm ($\frac{3}{8}$ in) beehive*	orange
	10	12 cm (4 $\frac{3}{4}$ in)	10 mm ($\frac{3}{8}$ in) beehive*	pale orange
	14	12 cm (4 $\frac{3}{4}$ in)	beehive	sage green

*The finished length of the 10 mm ($\frac{3}{8}$ in) beehives should be 2–2.5 cm (approx. 1 in).

To make the flowerets insert each 5 cm (2 in) fringed lemon tight coil into an 8 cm (3 in) sage green beehive. Glue together. Take six of the flowerets and glue their bases together to make each of the two open flower sprays. Gently spread out the fringes with your fingertips until the flower sprays resemble pom-poms. The three remaining flowerets are used for the buds.

    To make the buds take the 12 cm (4 ¾ in) orange and pale orange 10 mm

(⅜ in) beehives and insert each one into a 12 cm (4 ¾ in) sage green beehive. Glue together. Gently bend some of the long beehives to give them a curved shape. Referring to the illustration as necessary, make one large bud spray by gluing together the bases of seven buds and one floweret, and the other by gluing together the bases of seven buds and two flowerets, to make bud sprays that resemble alien spiders!

Arrangement

Position the 13 cm (5 in) stem onto your card so it is hanging down. Add a 5 mm (⁵⁄₁₆ in) leaf stem near the tip and position the two 30 cm (12 in) leaves at the end of this stem and at the tip. Position the remaining stems as desired. Place one of the bud sprays at the end of one of the 6 cm (2 ¼ in) stems and place a 60 cm (24 in) leaf at the end of the other 6 cm (2 ¼ in) stem. Overlap two of the leaves to add dimension.

Add remaining bud spray and the flowers.

Australian natives

Inspiration for quilling designs can come from many sources. All you need is a little imagination and creativity to see the basic shapes that make up the object, flower or animal. Inspiration for some of the following designs came from a catalogue of educational products. The original pictures were Aboriginal designs portrayed on wooden jigsaw puzzles for pre-schoolers and kindergarten age children. The pictures were colourful and adapted very well to the medium of quilling.

ECHIDNA
Tachyglossus aculeatus

The echidna is a shy creature so it is a rare treat to come across one in the wild. They are one of the only two egg-laying mammals in the world. The other is another Australian, the platypus. Echidnas love to feast on ants and termites and their snout and long sticky tongue are superbly designed for this purpose. Their powerful claws enable them to dig themselves into the ground very quickly when danger threatens. Unfortunately they don't have a lot of traffic sense and it is tragic to all too often see them dead on the side of the road.

Part	Quantity	Length	Shape	Colour
Body	1	120 cm (48 in)	teardrop	brown
Snout	1	30 cm (12 in)	eye	yellow
Feet	4	15 cm (6 in)	birdfoot	tan
Eyes	2	2 cm ($^3/_4$ in)	tight coil	white
Quills	34	5 mm ($^1/_4$ in)	strip	brown

Arrangement

Position the body of the echidna on the card and glue into place. Squeeze the snout as firmly as you can so it is long and thin. Add the snout, feet and eyes as illustrated and glue down. Lastly glue down the short brown strips, on edge, for the quills.

TURTLE
Chelonia sp.

Freshwater turtles differ from sea turtles in that they have clawed, webbed feet like a duck, rather than flippers, which enables them to move overland to find water after their swamp or creek has dried up. This characteristic means that freshwater turtles (which are amphibious) are often mistakenly referred to as tortoises (which are land-dwellers). Turtles used to be slaughtered in huge numbers, mainly for their meat. In the 1800s turtle soup was an incredibly expensive gourmet dish. Nowadays most, if not all, turtle species are protected.

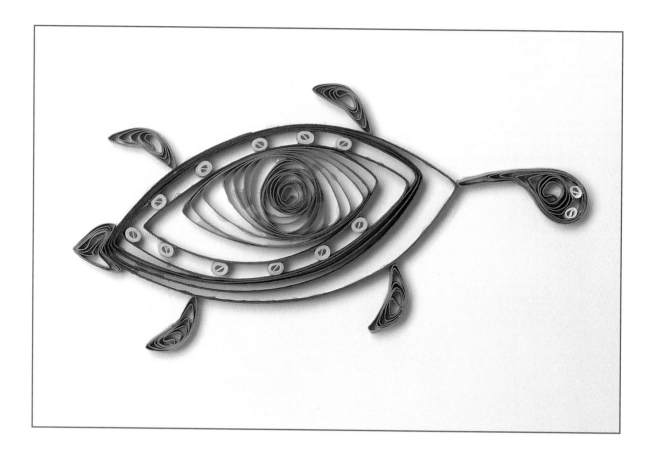

Part	Quantity	Length	Shape	Colour
Body	1	60 cm (24 in)	strip	green
	1	60 cm (24 in)	strip	brown
Feet	4	10 cm (4 in)	crescent	green
Tail	1	10 cm (4 in)	arrow	green
Head	1	25 cm (10 in)	bent teardrop	green
Eyes	2	1 cm ($^3/_8$ in)	tight coil	white
Spots	11	3 cm ($1^1/_8$ in)	tight coil	yellow

To make the body, glue the 60 cm (24 in) green strip to the 60 cm (24 in) brown strip, end to end. Commence rolling from the green end, into a loose coil, before squeezing to an eye shape.

Arrangement

Position the body of the turtle onto the card. Insert the yellow spots evenly between the coils of the body surrounding the centre. Add a dab of glue to each spot to hold it in place before glueing the whole body to the card. Add the legs and tail. Insert the eyes into the head before glueing it into place.

DANCING BROLGA
Grus rubicundus

The stately brolga belongs to a very old group of birds with fossil ancestors dating back millions of years. The brolga is particularly noted for its elaborate dancing, performed not only as a courtship ritual, but also outside the breeding season. The birds line up opposite one another and step forward, shaking their outstretched wings. They bob their heads and bow, and sometimes one will throw back its head and trumpet loudly. Occasionally one will leap a metre or so into the air and parachute back to the ground. Brolgas live in northern and eastern tropical areas of Australia, but have also been recorded in New Guinea and some Coral Sea Islands.

Part	Quantity	Length	Shape	Colour
Head	1	15 cm (6 in)	teardrop	red
Eye	1	5 cm (2 in)	tight coil	yellow
Beak	1	20 cm (8 in)	arrow	silver
Neck	1	30 cm (12 in)	arrow	grey
Body	1	60 cm (24 in)	eye	grey
Wings	2	30 cm (12 in)	crescent	grey
Feathers	4	20 cm (8 in)	crescent	grey
	16	10 cm (4 in)	eye	white
	12	15 cm (6 in)	eye	white
	11	20 cm (8 in)	eye	white
Legs	2	4 cm (1½ in)	strip	grey
Feet	2	20 cm (8 in)	birdfoot	grey

Arrangement

Glue the body to the card first, followed by the neck, head and beak. Insert the eye. Add the wings and feathers, with the smaller feathers at the top under the wings and the larger feathers at the bottom. The grey feathers should touch the wing tips at the outermost point. Fold the two 4 cm (1½ in) strips for the legs in half, creasing them firmly, then straighten them out to the desired angle before glueing them on each side of the body. Add the feet.

CROCODILE

The native amphibious Australian reptiles sometimes referred to alligators are in fact crocodiles. (Australia has no alligators except those in captivity.) Two species of crocodile dwell in the tropics of the Top End. The usually harmless Freshwater Crocodile, 2–3 metres (7–10 feet) long, is Crocodylus johnstoni; *the larger and much more dangerous Estuarine or Saltwater Crocodile, 3–5 metres (10–17 feet) long, is* Crocodylus porosus. *Don't be misled by the name into thinking you will only see the larger beastie in salt water, however, for the salties enjoy fresh water as well. And as the song says, 'Never smile at a crocodile …*

Part	Quantity	Length	Shape	Colour
Head (teardrop)*	1	15 cm (6 in)	strip	yellow
	1	10 cm (4 in)	strip	cream
Body (crescent)*	1	40 cm (16 in)	strip	yellow
	1	20 cm (8 in)	strip	cream
Tail (leaf)*	1	35 cm (14 in)	strip	yellow
	1	15 cm (6 in)	strip	cream
Legs (eye)*	4	10 cm (4 in)	strip	yellow
	4	5 cm (2 in)	strip	cream
Feet (birdfoot)*	4	1 cm ($^3/_8$ in)	strip	yellow
	4	3 cm ($1^1/_8$ in)	strip	cream
Eyes	2	2 cm ($^3/_4$ in)	tight coil	grey
Circles	4	30 cm (12 in)	loose coil	yellow
	52	5 cm (2 in)	tight coil	cream

*To make these parts of the crocodile, join the cream and yellow strips together end to end to make a longer strip. Commencing at the yellow end, roll each length into a loose coil and squeeze to the required shape.

Arrangement

Position the parts of the crocodile on your card as illustrated, keeping in mind the fact that none of the parts are actually touching each other. Glue into place. Arrange a yellow circle in each corner of the card and surround it with 13 cream tight coils. Glue to the card.

CARPET PYTHON
Morelia spilota

One of Australia's best-known snake species is the Carpet Python, so named for its beautiful patterns. Non-poisonous, unlike many other Australian snakes, the Carpet Python comes in a wide range of colour forms and markings; often in greys and browns and creams, intricately spotted and banded, sometimes bright green all over. Two of the more spectacular varieties are the Diamond Python (Morelia spilota spilota), found in the cooler south-eastern states, and the Jungle Carpet Python (Morelia spilota cheynei), a tree-dweller from the rainforests of north-east Queensland. If a carpet python takes up residence in your roof, or under the house, relax—it is perfectly harmless and will eat any intruding rats and mice.

Part	Quantity	Length	Shape	Colour
Body	1	120 cm (48 in)	strip	bright green
Eyes	2	2 cm (3/4 in)	tight coil	cream
Pattern	62	2 cm (3/4 in)	tight coil	cream
	97	2 cm (3/4 in)	tight coil	yellow
	1	80 cm (32 in)	strip	bright green
Leaves	14	10 cm (4 in)	bent teardrop	bright green

Take the 80 cm (32 in) bright green strip and fold it every 5 mm (5/16 in) in the opposite direction so it stretches and contracts like a concertina.

Arrangement

Take the long strip for the body and, dabbing glue on the edge a section at a time, arrange on the card to form a curvy snake shape with a pointed tail and definite head. Trim any excess strip. Decorate inside the body with the green concertina strip, and the cream and yellow tight coils. Add eyes. Place the leaves randomly on the card surrounding the python. I chose a dark background to simulate night-time for the stylised version of this nocturnal hunter.

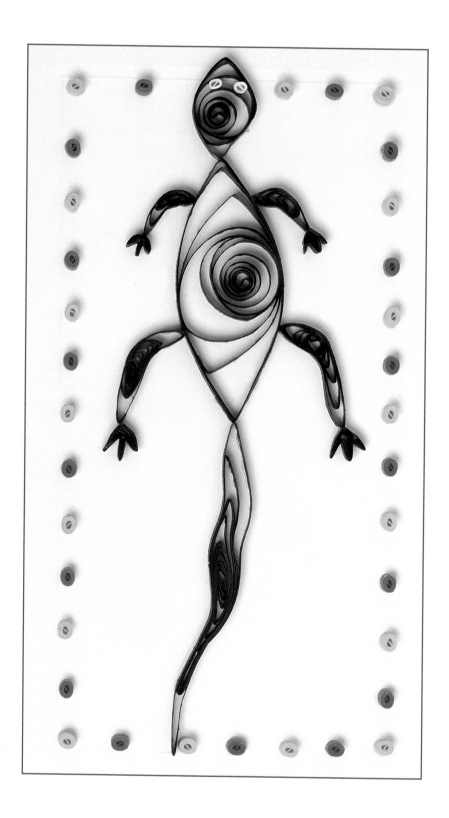

PERENTIE
Varanus giganteus

Australia is home to many different types of lizards, from small geckos and skinks, to the medium-sized and showy Thorny Devil and Frill-neck Lizard, to the large goannas reminiscent of the days of the dinosaur. The largest goanna, the beautifully patterned Perentie, measuring up to 2 metres (7 feet) long, is the third largest lizard in the world. Goannas are generally not aggressive unless cornered, and their preferred route of escape is up a tree. People standing still have been known to be mistaken for a tree by a frightened goanna, and have received quite deep scratches from the animal's attempt to climb them.

Part	Quantity	Length	Shape	Colour
Head	1	20 cm (8 in)	eye	black
Body	1	60 cm (24 in)	eye	black
Tail	1	60 cm (24 in)	leaf	black
Eyes	2	2 cm ($^3/_4$ in)	tight coil	cream
Legs	2	10 cm (4 in)	crescent	black
	2	20 cm (8 in)	crescent	black
Claws	2	10 cm (4 in)	birdfoot	black
	2	6 cm ($2^1/_4$ in)	birdfoot	black
Border	17	5 cm (2 in)	tight coil	yellow
	17	5 cm (2 in)	tight coil	red

Arrangement

Position the body, head and tail of the goanna on the card. Add the two shorter legs at the front and the two longer legs at the back of the body. The smaller claws join onto the end of the front legs, the larger claws join to the end of the back legs. Insert the eyes into the head. When you are satisfied with the arrangement, glue all the parts to the card. Evenly space and alternate the yellow and red tight coils to make a rectangular border around the goanna.

WATER LIFE

Australia, being surrounded by ocean and with extensive inland waterways, has a rich and diverse variety of saltwater and freshwater creatures. There are brightly coloured tropical fish, spiky sea urchins, soft sponges, sharp corals, walking mud-fish, stinging jellies and man-eating sharks, to name but a few. I chose to quill an unusual collection of water-dwellers, with a colourful starfish and a manta ray—giant of all stingrays and yet the most harmless—from the ocean, and every child's favourite, freshwater tadpoles!

Part	Quantity	Length	Shape	Colour
Manta ray				
Body	1	30 cm (12 in)	teardrop	dark green
Wings	2	45 cm (18 in)	triangle	dark green
Tail	1	45 cm (18 in)	bent teardrop	dark green
Horns	2	5 cm (2 in)	crescent	dark green
Eyes	2	5 cm (2 in)	tight coil	white
Starfish				
Body	1	20 cm (8 in)	loose coil	orange
Arms	5	45 cm (18 in)	leaf	magenta
Tadpoles				
Body	7	10 cm (4 in)	eye	brown
Tail	7	1 cm ($^3/_8$ in)	strip	brown

To make the manta ray glue the wings to each side of the body. Then add the tail (squeezed very flat and curved). Position the horns at the front of the body. Place the eyes on top of the intersections between the body and the horns.

To make the starfish squeeze the arms very flat and glue them around the body, radiating outwards.

To make the tadpoles bend each tail to an S-shape, then glue them to one end of each body.

Arrangement

Position the manta ray in one corner of your card, and the starfish diagonally opposite. The tadpoles form a line swimming between the two. I made the tadpoles in a traditional brown but they can be any colour you choose.

Christmas

While commercially produced Christmas cards are easily purchased in bulk for very little expense, in this high-speed technological age it is delightful to receive a unique hand-made card. People who are too busy or don't have the inclination to make their own Christmas cards appreciate the time and care that goes into hand-made ones. Here are just a few designs to make and send to the special people in your life.

NAIVE CHRISTMAS TREE

This simple tree is quilled in the style of a child's drawing—three green triangles one above the other with spots for baubles and a yellow star on top. Nowadays many Christmas trees are designer creations with all of the decorations carefully arranged and colour coordinated. I still love to adorn my tree with the decorations the kids made at pre-school, no matter that some of them are falling to bits and no two are the same. There are so many memories attached to each piece that they are all special.

Part	Quantity	Length	Shape	Colour
Star	1	10 cm (4 in)	star	yellow
Baubles	6	10 cm (4 in)	tight coil	red
Branches	1	25 cm (10 in)	triangle	green
	1	30 cm (12 in)	triangle	green
	1	40 cm (16 in)	triangle	green
Trunk	1	10 cm (4 in)	eye	brown

Arrangement

Arrange the three green triangles one above the other to form a Christmas tree shape, with the smallest triangle at the top and the largest at the bottom. Glue into place. Squeeze the trunk firmly until it is almost flat. Decorate the tree by placing the star at the top, and a red bauble at the end of each branch. If you wish to put your tree into a pot, cut the required shape from a piece of coloured card and either glue it or fasten it to the card with double-sided mounting tape.

FESTIVE MICE

These cheeky mice are having their own Christmas feast on a wedge of Swiss cheese. They are quite appealing with their Santa hats perched rakishly on their heads—unlike the real specimens, who invade my house every now and them, leaving behind their little black calling cards and mousy odour. Interestingly, when trying to trap mice I have found bread to be a far better bait than cheese.

Part	Quantity	Length	Shape	Colour
Body	4	30 cm (12 in)	teardrop	grey
Head	4	15 cm (6 in)	teardrop	grey
Ear	4	7 cm (2¾ in)	teardrop	grey
Eye	4	2 cm (¾ in)	tight coil	pink
Tail	4	3 cm (1⅛ in)	strip	grey
Hat	4	10 cm (4 in)	triangle	red
Pompom	4	5 cm (2 in)	tight coil	white
Christmas cheese	1	60 cm (24 in)	triangle	yellow
	5	10 cm (4 in)	tight coil	yellow
Crumbs	3	2 cm (¾ in)	triangle	yellow

Arrangement

Insert the yellow tight coils into the cheese so they represent the holes in Swiss cheese and glue onto your card. Scatter the crumbs and arrange the mice around the cheese.

CHRISTMAS CANDLE

A candle centrepiece on the dining table at Christmas adds a lovely peaceful atmosphere. In Australia, Christmas is celebrated during the hottest part of the summer and the candles are inclined to bend and droop in the heat or burn to one side from the breeze of the air-conditioner or fan.

Part	Quantity	Length	Shape	Colour
Candle	1	120 cm (48 in)	teardrop	white
Flame	1	8 cm (3 in)	teardrop	yellow
Holly	5	40 cm (16 in)	holly	green
	2	30 cm (12 in)	holly	green
	1	25 cm (10 in)	holly	green
Berries	15	10 cm (4 in)	tight coil	red

You may need to glue two or three white strips together end to end to make a 120 cm (48 in) length for the candle.

Arrangement

Arrange the five large holly leaves on the card so they all point to a cluster of berries at the centre. Place the candle above the leaves and berries and put the flame at the top. Glue everything to the card. Then put the three remaining leaves on top of the first layer, again around a few berries at the centre. Glue into place. The finished design should look somewhat like the centrepiece for a table decoration.

DOVE OF PEACE

Although the dove bearing a branch of olive leaves in its beak is more correctly equated with the Biblical story of Noah and the flood, it is popularly used as an image on Christmas cards and other publications, and on the flag of the United Nations, as a symbol of peace.

Part	Quantity	Length	Shape	Colour
Body	1	40 cm (16 in)	teardrop	white
Head	1	15 cm (6 in)	loose coil	white
Wings	2	20 cm (8 in)	bent teardrop	white
Eye	1	2 cm (¾ in)	tight coil	yellow
Beak	1	2 cm (¾ in)	strip	yellow
Olive branch	1	2 cm (¾ in)	strip	brown
Leaves	5	5 cm (2 in)	teardrop	green

To make the beak, fold the 2 cm (¾ in) yellow strip in half and glue the fold to the head. Allow to dry before trimming with scissors to the required length.

Arrangement

Arrange the pieces of the dove on the card so it appears to be flying down towards the bottom left corner. When you are satisfied with the position, glue into place. Curve the brown strip for the olive branch and place at the end of the beak. Add the leaves.

POINSETTIA
Euphorbia pulcherrima

This Mexican native shrub was discovered by Joel Roberts Poinsett in 1828. At the time he was the first US Ambassador to Mexico, appointed by President Andrew Jackson. The Aztecs in the fourteenth to sixteenth centuries used the milky sap of this plant to control fevers, and the colourful bracts were used to make a reddish dye. Traditionally poinsettias are red but there are also pink or white varieties. Contrary to common belief, poinsettias are not poisonous, but their milky sap can be irritating to the skin and cause temporary blindness if it gets in the eye. Poinsettias are the top selling potted plant in the United States, where December 12 is National Poinsettia Day.

Part	Quantity	Length	Shape	Colour
Flower 1				
Flower centres	5	6 cm (2¼ in)	strip	red
	5	4 cm (1½ in)	strip	yellow
	5	1 cm (³⁄₈ in)	sliver	red
Leaves	6	30 cm (12 in)	holly	sage green
Bracts	6	10 cm (4 in)	eye	red
	6	15 cm (6 in)	eye	red

Flower 2 is the same as Flower 1.

To make the flower centres, join a 6 cm (2¼ in) red strip to a 4 cm (1½ in) yellow strip end to end. When the glue is dry, start from the red end and roll into a tight coil. Cut a sliver of red paper and insert it into the centre of the tight coil. Add a dab of glue to hold it in place. Trim the sliver with scissors so it protrudes a little way out of the tight coil.

Arrangement

Referring to the illustration as necessary, arrange the six leaves with their points towards the centre. Glue to the card. Place the six larger bracts on top of the leaves, also with their points meeting in the centre, and glue into place. Place the flower centres on top of the large bracts and glue down. Add the six smaller bracts radiating out from the flower centres.

Make the second flower the same way. If your card is big enough you may like to add more flowers.

WORSHIP OF THE MAGI

'They went into the house, and when they saw the child with his mother Mary, they knelt and worshipped him. They brought out their gifts of gold, frankincense and myrrh, and presented them to him.' Matthew 2:11, Good News Bible.

This design is an abstract interpretation of the wise men worshipping the baby Jesus. The robes of the wise men can be any colour you prefer. I chose rich colours, imagining the fabric to be silk, but in reality they were more likely to have been wearing clothes of a much coarser material—which would have been covered in dust, sand, sweat and camel hair from the long journey through the desert.

Part	Quantity	Length	Shape	Colour
Star	1	60 cm (24 in)	diamond	yellow
Wise Man 1	1	15 cm (6 in)	bent teardrop	light tan
	2	25 cm (10 in)	leaf	magenta
	1	15 cm (6 in)	teardrop	magenta

Wise Men 2 and 3 are the same as 1, but their robes are different colours. I used purple and burgundy.

Part	Quantity	Length	Shape	Colour
Crown	3	10 cm (4 in)	birdfoot	yellow
Manger	1	25 cm (10 in)	half moon	brown
	1	2 cm ($^3/_4$ in)	strip	brown
Baby Jesus	1	10 cm (4 in)	half moon	cream

Arrangement

Position the star at the top left-hand corner of the card and glue into place. Below the star place the manger on its curved stand. Put the baby in the manger. To make the first wise man, start with the 15 cm (6 in) teardrop for the base. Add the leaf shape above the base so they join to make the robe. Position the bent teardrop so the point is touching the top of the robe and looks like a bowed head. Place the crown on top of the head. Do the same for the other two wise men—I squeezed the shapes slightly differently so that each wise man has a character of his own. The finished scene should look like the three wise men kneeling at the manger.

Floral emblems

Throughout the world symbols such as flags and national anthems are used to inspire their people to patriotism and pride. Many countries have a national holiday celebrating an important date in their history. Most countries also have a national flower or floral emblem, but these are usually less well known. Do you know the national flower of your country? States, counties and provinces often have floral emblems as well. Some countries have both an official floral emblem and a popular one. Here are just some of the flowers that have achieved international recognition for their country.

GOLDEN WATTLE
Acacia pycnantha

The Golden Wattle is the national floral emblem of Australia. It was officially proclaimed on 1 September 1988, by the then Governor-General of Australia, Sir Ninian Stephen, at a ceremony held in the national Botanic Gardens in Canberra. September 1 is Wattle Day in Australia. The Golden Wattle is a small shrubby tree ranging from 4 to 8 metres (13–25 feet) tall. It grows in the temperate regions of the country's south-eastern states. Like most acacias it is relatively short lived.

Part	Quantity	Length	Shape	Colour
Stem	1	11 cm (4¼ in)	strip	light brown
Leaves	5	30 cm (12 in)	eye	sage green
Flowers	23	5 cm (2 in) 10 mm (³/₈ in) strip	fringed	yellow

Roll each of the fringed strips for the flowers into a tight coil and glue. When dry, gently spread out the fringes with your fingers.

Squeeze the eye shapes for the leaves firmly so they are almost flat.

Arrangement
Position the stem on the card to hang down from the top left corner. Place the flowers and leaves randomly along the stem and glue into place. Add more or less leaves and flowers as desired.

KOWHAI
Sophora microphylla

The deciduous Kowhai (pronounced korfie) is native to New Zealand and is the floral emblem of that country. It grows to 10 metres (35 feet) tall and flowers in spring, between August and October. The leaves appear after flowering. The Maori people used parts of the kowhai for medicinal purposes, but careful preparation was essential to avoid the toxic alkaloids. The wood is hard and durable and was used for canoe paddles and adzes in earlier days. Modern uses include making fence posts. The honey-laden golden flowers are also popular with the birds.

Part	Quantity	Length	Shape	Colour
Branch	1	11 cm (4¼ in)	strip	light brown
Stems	7	assorted	strip	light brown
Leaves	26	5 cm (2 in)	loose coil	green
Flowers	3	30 cm (12 in)	leaf	yellow
	3	30 cm (12 in)	crescent	yellow
Buds	2	30 cm (12 in)	leaf	yellow
Caps	3	54 cm (21 in)	beehive	lemon
	2	30 cm (12 in)	beehive	lemon
Stamens	3	2 cm (¾ in)	strip	lemon

Construct the flowers first. Glue the sides of a 30 cm (12 in) yellow crescent and a 30 cm (12 in) yellow leaf together so they are joined halfway down. Then glue the joined end into a 54 cm (21 in) yellow beehive. Take the short strip for the stamen and cut three slits into it lengthways. Glue it to the flower at the join of the crescent and leaf. Do the same for the other flowers.

To construct the buds, glue one end of the 30 cm (12 in) leaf shapes into the 30 cm (12 in) caps.

Arrangement

Position the branch on the card and glue down. Place the longer stems so they are joined to the branch and add leaves. Glue into place. Add the remaining short stems and place a flower or bud at the end of each. Overlapping the flowers adds dimension to your card. Be sure to glue them down securely.

HONG KONG ORCHID TREE
Bauhinia blakeana

Bauhinia blakeana *is the showiest of the Bauhinias and has been the floral emblem of Hong Kong since 1965. Flowering during winter, its blooms are generally a spectacular reddish purple but it can also have white forms. As with all Bauhinias it has leaves shaped like a butterfly, a heart or a camel's hoof, depending on your point of view. The Hong Kong Orchid Tree is propagated by means of cuttings, as its seeds are sterile. It was first officially described in 1908 and named in honour of Sir Henry Blake, Governor of Hong Kong from 1898 to 1903.*

Part	Quantity	Length	Shape	Colour
Main stem	1	13 cm (5 in)	strip	green
Bud stems	1	3.5 cm (1 ³/₈ in)	strip	green
	1	2 cm (³/₄ in)	strip	green
Flower stems	3	2 cm (1 in)	strip	green
Leaf stems	3	1 cm (³/₈ in)	strip	green
	3	5 mm (⁵/₁₆ in)	strip	green
Leaves	2	15 cm (6 in)	crescent	green
	5	12 cm (4 ³/₄ in)	crescent	green
Buds	4	10 cm (4 in)	half-moon	green
	2	12 cm (4 ³/₄ in)	half-moon	green
Flowers	20	15 cm (6 in)	eye	magenta
	5	20 cm (8 in)	eye	magenta
Stamens	5	1 cm (³/₈ in)	fringed	magenta

10 mm (³/₈ in) tight coil

To make the flowers squeeze the eye shapes so they are longer and more pointed at one end than the other. There are five eyes per flower. Glue the longer pointed ends together to form the flower centre. Make four small flowers and one larger flower in this manner. Glue the stamens on top of the centre. I added a dab of white paint to the tips of the stamens.

Arrangement

Turn your blank card to the horizontal. Position the 13 cm (5 in) stem across the card so it looks as if it is branching slightly upwards. Place one small flower at the top end of the stem. Place the two bud stems branching upwards from the main stem and add four buds to the longer stem and two buds to the shorter one. Position the three remaining small flowers lower down the main stem and just above it, grouped closely together. Add their stems and glue into position. Take the large flower and glue it on top of the main stem and the flower stems to give a three-dimensional effect. Position the remaining leaves as desired.

ROSE
Rosa sp.

The rose is the floral emblem of several countries, including England, the United States, Bulgaria, Cyprus, Czechoslovakia and Iran, to name but a few. Roses come in many colours—reds, yellows, pinks, whites, and even stripes. The perfume of a rose garden in the early summer evening is quite heady; no wonder the rose is so closely associated with love.

Part	Quantity	Length	Shape	Colour
Flowers	6	20 cm (8 in)	10 mm ($^3/_8$ in) strip	pink
Leaves	15	10 cm (4 in)	eye	green
Flower stems	1	10 cm (4 in)	strip	green
	1	8 cm (3 in)	strip	green
	1	2 cm ($^3/_4$ in)	strip	green
Leaf stems	5	2 cm ($^3/_4$ in)	strip	green

Make the rose flowers according to the instructions at the beginning of the book.

Arrangement

Arrange the flower stems on the card and glue into place. Arrange the leaf stems so they are branching off the flower stems and glue down. Add three leaves to each leaf stem. Add flowers, one at the end of each flower stem and the remainder randomly along the stems. Glue firmly to the card.

TULIP
Tulipa sp.

Whenever I think of tulips, I imagine them in fields with Dutch windmills nearby. It is not surprising that the tulip is indeed the floral emblem of the Netherlands. The tulip is not native to the Netherlands, in fact it originates from Persia and Turkey. It is also the national flower of Turkey. The tulip was introduced into Holland in the sixteenth century during the time of the Ottoman Empire. Although the origin of the name Tulip is unknown, one explanation is that it is named after its resemblance to the turban, the headgear worn by many Persians and Turks. The Latin for turban is tulipa.

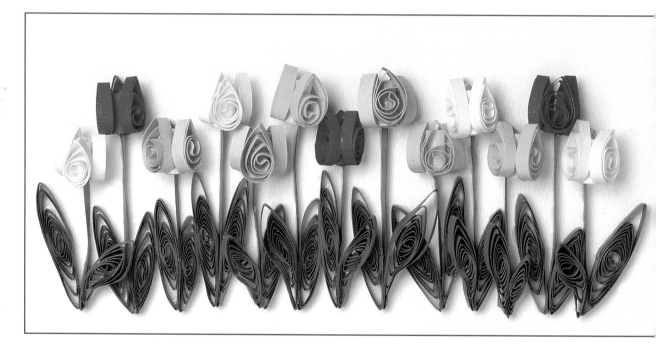

Part	Quantity	Length	Shape	Colour
Flowers	3	10 cm (4 in)	10 mm (3/8 in) tight coil	pink
	9	10 cm (4 in)	teardrop	pink
	3	10 cm (4 in)	10 mm (3/8 in) tight coil	red
	9	10 cm (4 in)	teardrop	red
	3	10 cm (4 in)	10 mm (3/8 in) tight coil	yellow
	9	10 cm (4 in)	teardrop	yellow
	4	10 cm (4 in)	10 mm (3/8 in) tight coil	white
	12	10 cm (4 in)	teardrop	white
Leaves	13	30 cm (12 in)	eye	green
	10	25 cm (10 in)	eye	green
	3	20 cm (8 in)	eye	green
Stems	7	3 cm (1 1/8 in)	strip	green
	6	4 cm (1 1/2 in)	strip	green

To make the tulip flowers, take the 10 mm (3/8 in) wide tight coil and glue three teardrops of the matching colour around it, making sure that the bases of the teardrops are level with the base of the tight coil. The squeezed end of the teardrops should point upwards. Do this for each flower until you have 13 flowers.

Arrangement

Arrange the stems in a row on the card, alternating the two different lengths, and glue them on edge to the card. Place a flower at the top of each stem and glue down. Add a leaf to both sides of each stem. You may need to bend and overlap some leaves to make them fit; this will add extra dimension to your arrangement. Glue firmly to card. Mix colours together as shown or try a mass planting of just one colour.

TWIN-FLOWER
Linnea borealis

This flower is the floral emblem of Sweden. It gets its common name from the fact that each stem bears two flowers. The fragrant bell-shaped flowers are quite small, about the size of a large fly. The flower is named in honour of Carl Linneaus, the Swedish scientist who founded the modern classification of plant species. In Sweden Linnea is also a popular name for girls.

Part	Quantity	Length	Shape	Colour
Flowers	5	60 cm (24 in)	strip	pink
	5	6 cm (2¼ in)	strip	green
	18	10 cm (4 in)	bent teardrop	white
Bud	1	60 cm (24 in)	strip	pink
	1	6 cm (2¼ in)	strip	green
	1	50 cm (20 in)	tight coil	pink
Leaves	24	10 cm (4 in)	teardrop	green
Stems	3	7 cm (2¾ in)	strip	green
	1	8 cm (3 in)	strip	green
	1	5 cm (2 in)	strip	green
	1	4 cm (1½ in)	strip	green

To make the flowers, join a 60 cm (24 in) pink strip to a 6 cm (2¼ in) green strip. Starting from the green end, roll into a beehive. Take three or four of the white bent teardrops and glue the bent ends around half of the inside edge of the beehive. Make five flowers in this manner.

To make the bud, join the 60 cm (24 in) pink strip to the 6 cm (2¼ in) green strip. Starting from the green end, roll into a beehive. Take the 50 cm (20 in) pink tight coil and glue it inside the open end of the beehive so it fits like a lid.

Arrangement

Referring to the illustration, fold the three 7 cm (2¾ in) stems in half to form V shapes, then fold a short section of the tops of the V outwards. Arrange these on the card. Add a stem to the bottom of the V, and glue down firmly. Add the flowers and the bud to the tops of the folded stems so they hang like bells. Add leaves, placing three or four at the base of each stem and the rest as random rosettes.

RHODODENDRON
Rhododendron arboreum

Over 800 species of rhododendron are native to a wide part of the northern hemisphere, many of them found in western China and the Himalayas. Rhododendron arboreum, *known locally as Lali Guras or Rose Tree, is the national flower of Nepal. I can remember as a child going with my parents to visit the National Rhododendron Gardens at Olinda in Victoria. The rhododendron and azalea blooms were just superb although I didn't appreciate them at the time. Now that I live in a climate that is hot, dry and dusty, I long to be able to visit those cool lush gardens again and soak up the beauty of these magnificent cool climate flowers.*

Part	Quantity	Length	Shape	Colour
Flower 1	23	30 cm (12 in)	beehive	red
Flower 2	23	30 cm (12 in)	beehive	red
Leaves	4	30 cm (12 in)	eye	green
	4	45 cm (18 in)	eye	green
Stems	2	8 cm (3 in)	strip	brown

To make the flowers, arrange 11 of the red beehives side by side into a circle with the pointed ends towards the centre. Glue them together. Add eight beehives on top of the first layer in the same manner. The remaining four beehives go on top, points toward the centre, creating a dome-shaped flower. No points should now be visible.

Arrangement

Arrange the stems on the card so one is branching off the other, and glue into place. Place a flower at the top of each stem. Add two large and two small leaves to the top of each stem underneath the flower, positioning them so they are hanging down. When you are satisfied with your arrangement, glue all the pieces into place.

QUEEN OF THE LAELIAS
Laelia purpurata

This magnificent orchid is the national flower of Brazil. It is the largest and probably the showiest of the genus Laelia. *Laelia orchids occur naturally in Mexico, Cuba and throughout South America. There are between 50 and 75 different species, the majority of them being found in Brazil. The genus* Laelia *is very closely related to* Cattleya, *and there is some discussion in the botanical world that several species should be reclassified as* Cattleya.

Part	Quantity	Length	Shape	Colour
Flower 1	5	30 cm (12 in)	eye	white
	1	25 cm (10 in)	strip	purple
	1	10 cm (4 in)	strip	yellow
Flower 2 is the same as flower 1.				
Leaves	2	60 cm (24 in)	eye	dark green
	1	50 cm (20 in)	eye	dark green

Join the 25 cm (10 in) purple strip to the 10 cm (4 in) yellow strip end to end. Starting from the yellow end, roll into a loose coil. Squeeze to a teardrop shape, making sure that the yellow part is at the pointed end.

Arrangement

Glue the leaves to the card in the desired position. Arrange the flowers above the leaves as illustrated. One of the flowers should slightly overlap the leaves. The purple 'tongue' of the flower is glued on top of the five white petals.

EDELWEISS

Leontopodium alpinum

This tiny but tough alpine flower is the floral emblem of both Switzerland and Austria. It leapt to international fame after being featured in the 1965 film, The Sound of Music. *My quilled interpretation is a good deal larger than life. The flower petals are not true petals, rather they are woolly bracts. The heads of the flowers look like lion's feet, hence their Latin name. Edelweiss grows best at high altitudes in the mountains of Europe.*

Part	Quantity	Length	Shape	Colour
Flower 1	5	20 cm (8 in)	teardrop	white
	5	10 cm (4 in)	teardrop	white
	1	10 cm (4 in)	strip	yellow
	1	5 cm (2 in)	strip	white
	7	6 cm (2$\frac{1}{4}$ in)	strip	yellow
	7	4 cm (1$\frac{1}{2}$ in)	strip	white

Flowers 2 and 3 are the same as flower 1.

Part	Quantity	Length	Shape	Colour
Leaves	15	30 cm (12 in)	eye	sage green
	11	20 cm (8 in)	eye	sage green
Stems	1	11 cm (4$\frac{1}{4}$ in)	strip	sage green
	1	8 cm (3 in)	strip	sage green
	1	5 cm (2 in)	strip	sage green

To make the flower, join together the 10 cm (4 in) yellow strip and the 5 cm (2 in) white strip end to end. Commencing at the yellow end, roll into a tight coil.

Join t the 6 cm (2¼ in) yellow strips to the 4 cm (1½ in) white strips to make seven 10 cm (4 in) strips. Commencing at the yellow end, roll each strip into a tight coil.

With the larger tight coil as the centre, glue the seven smaller tight coils around it. Then glue the 10 teardrops around the centre, alternating the large and small teardrops.

Make three flowers in this manner.

Arrangement

Take the fifteen 30 cm (12 in) leaves and divide into three groups of five. Arrange five leaves into a star shape on the card, with points touching in the centre. Do the same with the remaining leaves. When you are satisfied with your arrangement, glue to the card. Add the stems and the smaller leaves and glue to the card. Place each flower on top of a 'star' of leaves and glue on firmly.

Flower garden

Flowers, as far as I'm concerned, are definitely the easiest
objects to quill. There are so many different varieties in so
many shapes and colours that I am still finding new ones to
interpret in this medium. It is not always possible to capture
the subtle difference in shading of the petals, however, and
the speckled flowers are almost impossible unless you add a
finishing touch with a fine paintbrush. But their natural
shapes translate almost perfectly into quilled shapes and
I have enjoyed the challenge of creating these new designs for
you to use to decorate your next hand-made card.

BROMELIAD
Tillandsia cyanea

The common name for this flower is quite appropriate for the medium of this design. It is called Pink Quill. This bromeliad is one of the 374 species in the genus Tillandsia. *The plant originates from Ecuador, where it grows on tops of trees or shrubs that receive direct sun and high temperatures usually at altitudes of 330–1200 metres (1000–3500 feet). It bears only one or two blue or violet flowers at a time, over an extended period. Pink Quill grows very well in cultivation.*

Part	Quantity	Length	Shape	Colour
Flower	1	5 cm (2 in)	teardrop	mid-pink
	2	5 cm (2 in)	triangle	mid-pink
	2	10 cm (4 in)	triangle	mid-pink
	4	15 cm (6 in)	triangle	dark pink
	2	20 cm (8 in)	triangle	dark pink
	1	20 cm (8 in)	eye	dark pink
	2	25 cm (10 in)	triangle	dark pink
	2	10 cm (4 in)	teardrop	purple
	1	10 cm (4 in)	crescent	purple
Leaves	1	148 cm (60 in)	crescent	dark green
	2	74 cm (29 in)	crescent	dark green
	1	70 cm (28 in)	crescent	dark green
	2	60 cm (24 in)	crescent	dark green
	1	45 cm (18 in)	crescent	dark green
	1	35 cm (14 in)	crescent	dark green
	1	30 cm (12 in)	crescent	dark green

To make the flower, you will find it helpful to refer closely to the illustration. Start with the 5 cm (2 in) mid-pink teardrop. Add the two 5 cm (2 in) triangles, followed by the two 10 cm (4 in) triangles, two 15 cm (6 in) triangles, two 20 cm (8 in) triangles and two 25 cm (10 in) triangles, interlocking them neatly. Then add the remaining two 15 cm (6 in) triangles followed by the 20 cm (8 in) eye, which should be squeezed flat. Glue all these pieces together. Add the purple crescent and teardrops so they are coming out from between two of the dark pink triangles.

To make the leaves, bend all of the dark green crescents to different angles so that some are only slightly curved and others are quite acute.

Arrangement

Arrange the flower and leaves on the card in the desired position. When satisfied with the arrangement, glue firmly into place.

PURPLE CONE FLOWER
Echinacea purpurea

The Purple Cone Flower originates from North America. It is a perennial herb that can grow up to 1.50 metres (5 feet) tall. The medicinal properties of the flower have long been known to Native Americans, and now echinacea is a common ingredient in modern pharmaceutical remedies worldwide, particularly for relieving the symptoms of colds and flu.

Part	Quantity	Length	Shape	Colour
Flower 1	1	20 cm (8 in)	fringed 10 mm ($^3/_8$ in) strip	dark pink
	3	20 cm (8 in)	eye	dark pink
	2	20 cm (8 in)	leaf	dark pink
Flowers 2 and 3 are the same as Flower 1.				
Leaves	2	20 cm (8 in)	leaf	dark green
	3	15 cm (6 in)	leaf	dark green
Stems	1	10 cm (4 in)	strip	dark green
	1	9 cm (3$^1/_2$ in)	strip	dark green
	1	7 cm (2$^3/_4$ in)	strip	dark green

Roll the 20 cm (8 in) fringed strip into a tight coil and glue. When dry, gently spread out the fringes with your fingers.

Arrangement

Position the stems on edge on the card as desired. Place a fringed tight coil at the top of each stem. Add three pink eye shapes to 'hang' from the fringed tight coil. Place a pink leaf shape either side of the eyes. These shapes do not have to touch each other. Glue into place. Place the two larger leaves at the base of the main stem and position the remaining leaves randomly along the stems.

JAPONICA

Chaenomeles lagunaria

Japonica or Flowering Quince is a cool climate plant. It flowers in winter when the twigs, which are popular in flower arrangements, are usually bare of leaves. The flower buds will continue to open for several weeks if the cut twig is placed in a vase of water. Flowering occurs on the old wood so plants should not be pruned until after the blooms are finished. The flowers can be red, pink, apricot, crimson or white. Japonica originates from China and Japan.

Part	Quantity	Length	Shape	Colour
Flowers	5	3 cm (1⅛ in)	fringed 10 mm (³⁄₈ in) strip	white
	5	30 cm (12 in)	beehive	green
	25	10 cm (4 in)	teardrop	white
Buds	4	30 cm (12 in)	beehive	green
	4	20 cm (8 in)	beehive	white
Leaves	2	10 cm (4 in)	bent teardrop	green
Stem	1	14 cm (1½ in)	strip	brown

Roll the 3 cm (1⅛ in) fringed strip into a tight coil and glue. When dry, slightly spread out the fringes with your fingers. Glue inside a green beehive. Glue five white teardrops around the edge of the beehive so the points are touching the fringed centre. Do the same for the remaining flowers. As an added touch you may like to brush the tips of the fringes with gold paint or a gold felt-tipped pen.

To make the buds, flatten the white beehives until they are nicely rounded rather than pointed. Glue a white beehive inside a green beehive with the rounded side outwards.

Arrangement

Position the stem on edge on the card so it is angled from the bottom left corner to the opposite top corner. Place a bud at the top end of the stem and the remaining buds along both sides of the stem near the top. Add the flowers along both sides of the stem near the middle, placing them at different angles. Finally add the leaves near the base of the stem. Glue all pieces firmly to the card.

DWARF UMBRELLA TREE
Schefflera aboricola

The Dwarf Umbrella Tree is a hardy container plant. I have one on my verandah and it always looks good despite my dry, hot, dusty climate. It receives no direct sunlight and very little attention from me other than an occasional watering. Dwarf Umbrella Trees are often seen in corporate offices, banks and shopping centres, where they create a cool leafy atmosphere without taking over the place. I haven't seen them in flower, so this design only portrays the foliage, which is attractive enough by itself.

Part	Quantity	Length	Shape	Colour
Leaves	46	15 cm (6 in)	eye	green
Stems	42	2.5 cm (1 in)	strip	green
	3	3 cm (1⅛ in)	strip	green
	3	2 cm (¾ in)	strip	green
Main stem	1	14 cm (1½ in)	strip	green

Arrangement

Position the main stem on edge onto your card so it is angled from the bottom left corner to the opposite top corner. Glue into place. Starting from the bottom, place the 3 cm (1⅛ in) stems so they are branching off the main stem on alternating sides. Do the same with the 2 cm (¾ in) stems. At the end of each stem place seven of the 25 mm stems, radiating out like a star. Attach a leaf to the end of each of these until you have six fronds with seven leaves each. Put the remaining four leaves at the top of the main stem, so they look as if they are hanging down. Overlapping some of the leaves will add dimension to your card.

COOKTOWN ORCHID
Dendrobium bigibbum

Purists will no doubt dispute that this is a true and correct interpretation of the Cooktown Orchid, so I will have to request to be allowed some artistic licence! Flowers seem to vary in colour from pink to various shades of purple. The plant is native to Queensland and is also that state's floral emblem. The Cooktown Orchid is epiphytic rather than terrestrial, meaning that it grows on trees and not in soil on the ground. It was first collected in Australia from Mount Adolphus Island in the Torres Strait and subsequently named in 1852.

Part	Quantity	Length	Shape	Colour
Flower 1	2	15 cm (6 in)	teardrop	purple
	3	10 cm (4 in)	eye	purple
	1	10 cm (4 in)	arrow	purple
	1	20 cm (8 in)	beehive	purple

Flowers 2 and 3 are the same as Flower 1.

Part	Quantity	Length	Shape	Colour
Buds	2	10 cm (4 in)	arrow	purple
Leaves	3	30 cm (12 in)	crescent	dark green
	1	10 cm (4 in)	eye	dark green
Flower stems	3	1 cm ($^3/_8$ in)	strip	light brown
	2	5 mm ($^5/_{16}$ in)	strip	light brown
Main stem	1	14 cm ($1^1/_2$ in)	strip	light brown

To make the centre and lip of the flower glue the 10 cm (4 in) arrow to the side of the 20 cm (8 in) beehive. Make sure that the arrow is rounded rather than pointed at the end.

Arrangement

Position the main stem on edge so it curves across the card. Glue into place. Add the leaves at the bottom end of the stem. Place the two shorter flower stems towards the other end of the main stem pointing upwards. Put a bud at the end of each of these. Place the three 1 cm ($^3/_8$ in) stems along the main stem pointing upwards. Arrange a flower at the end of each of these. Glue everything firmly to your card.

SOLDIER LILY
Lachenalia tricolor

This colourful member of the Lily family originates from the Cape of Good Hope in South Africa. It is commonly called the Cape Cowslip as well as the Soldier Lily. It is named in honour of the Swiss botanist Professor Werner de Lachenal, who was professor of Botany at Basel in Switzerland in the late eighteenth century. Lachenalias grow best in small pots with good drainage and full to partial light. They are frost tender and prefer a temperate climate.

Part	Quantity	Length	Shape	Colour
Flowers	11	30 cm (12 in)	beehive	yellow
	3	20 cm (8 in)	beehive	red
	7	10 cm (4 in)	beehive	red
Leaves	5	20 cm (8 in)	eye	green
	1	60 cm (24 in)	leaf	green
	2	60 cm (24 in)	crescent	green
	2	30 cm (12 in)	eye	green
Stems	1	12 cm ($4^3/_4$ in)	strip	light brown
	1	11 cm ($4^1/_4$ in)	strip	light brown
	1	10 cm (4 in)	strip	light brown

Arrangement

Position the three stems on edge pointing upwards on the card. Glue into place. Add the leaves at the bottom of the stems, overlapping some. Put the small red flowers at the top of the stems (2, 3, 2), with a larger red flower beneath. Place the yellow flowers down each side of the stems until you are satisfied with the arrangement. Glue everything firmly to the card.

FLAMINGO FLOWER
Anthurium scherzerianum

The Flamingo Flower or Tail-flower, as it is also called, is a tropical perennial plant that originates from Central and South America. It requires humidity and full or partial shade, making it an ideal greenhouse plant. The shiny spathe can be red, salmon or pink and the spadix is usually yellow or white. The leaves are a dark leathery green. All parts of this showy and attractive plant are toxic if eaten.

Part	Quantity	Length	Shape	Colour
Flowers	2	60 cm (24 in)	arrow	red
	2	20 cm (8 in)	crescent	lemon
Bud	1	60 cm (24 in)	teardrop	red
Leaves	1	70 cm (28 in)	teardrop	dark green
	1	60 cm (24 in)	teardrop	dark green
	1	45 cm (18 in)	teardrop	dark green
	3	30 cm (12 in)	bent teardrop	dark green
	4	20 cm (8 in)	bent teardrop	dark green
Stems	1	7 cm (2¾ in)	strip	dark green
	2	5 cm (2 in)	strip	dark green
	1	4 cm (1½ in)	strip	dark green
	1	3 cm (1⅛ in)	strip	dark green

To make the flowers, glue the lemon crescents on top of the red arrows so they are curving up and outwards. Make sure the arrow shapes are rounded so they are more like a heart shape.

Glue a 5 cm (2 in) stem to the bud.

Arrangement

Position the two largest leaves approximately in the middle of the card pointing upwards. Place one flower between them so it is directly on the card. Glue into place. Add the stems on edge so they all meet at the bottom of the card. Place five of the smaller leaves around the base of the stems, pointing downwards and sideways. Put the 45 cm (18 in) leaf next to the large leaves. Place the other flower on top of the 45 cm (18 in) leaf. Put the bud with the point upward on top of the largest leaf, making sure the stem meets the other stems. Lastly, put the two remaining small leaves on top of the other small leaves so they are covering the point where the stems join. Glue everything firmly to the card.

SLIPPER ORCHID
Paphiopedilum insigne

So named because of their resemblance in shape to a lady's slipper, many slipper orchids are beautifully patterned with speckled petals. It is not possible to replicate this in quilling so I have chosen a plainer flower. This species is native to Assam, India and Nepal. It grows at an altitude of 1,000–1,500 metres (3,300–5,000 feet). It was discovered by Europeans in the early 1800s and specimens sent to England, where they flowered in the Liverpool Botanical Gardens in 1820.

Part	Quantity	Length	Shape	Colour
Flowers	2	120 cm (48 in)	beehive	yellow
	2	20 cm (8 in)	tight coil	yellow
	4	60 cm (24 in)	crescent	yellow
	2	25 cm (10 in)	strip	yellow
	2	15 cm (6 in)	strip	white
	2	20 cm (8 in)	strip	yellow
	2	10 cm (4 in)	strip	white
Leaves	2	30 cm (12 in)	teardrop	green
	3	60 cm (24 in)	teardrop	green
Stems	1	6 cm (2¼ in)	strip	green
	1	5 cm (2 in)	strip	green

To make the upper petal, join the 25 cm (10 in) yellow strip and the 15 cm (6 in) white strip end to end to make a 40 cm (16 in) length. Commencing at the yellow end, roll into a loose coil. Squeeze to a teardrop shape. Make two of these.

Join together the 20 cm (8 in) yellow strip and the 10 cm (4 in) white strip to make a 30 cm (12 in) length. Commencing at the yellow end, roll into a loose coil. Squeeze to a teardrop shape. Make two of these.

Arrangement

Arrange the stems as desired on the card. Add leaves at the base of the stems. At the top of the stems place the 30 cm (12 in) yellow and white teardrop, point down touching the stem. Take the yellow crescent shapes and put two on each flower, pointing to the sides. Add the 40 cm (16 in) yellow and white teardrop above the crescents, point toward the centre of the flower. Glue everything onto the card. Take the tight coil and glue it just inside the edge of the beehive. Then glue the beehive on its side on top of the smaller teardrop. Make sure the opening is at the centre of the flower with the cone part pointing down toward the stem. Glue firmly.

GERBERA
Gerbera jamesonii

The Gerbera or African Daisy is a perennial plant native to South Africa. They flower in a range of colours from orange, yellow and red to white, purple and pink. Gerberas have large flowers, sometimes up to 12 cm (4¾ in) across, and are very popular with florists as they have a long vase life, lasting up to two weeks. The genus Gerbera *is named after the German naturalist Traugott Gerber. There are approximately thirty species of gerbera to be found in Africa, Madagascar, South America and tropical Asia. Gerberas do not like cold climates.*

Part	Quantity	Length	Shape	Colour
Flower		1	10 cm (4 in)	strip pale orange
	1	5 cm (2 in)	fringed 10 mm ($^3/_8$ in) strip	orange
	11	30 cm (12 in)	eye	orange
Stem	1	11 cm (4$^1/_4$ in)	strip	dark green
Leaves	1	60 cm (24 in)	holly	dark green
	1	70 cm (28 in)	holly	dark green

Arrangement

Join together the 10 cm (4 in) pale orange strip and the 5 cm (2 in) fringed 10 mm (⅜ in) orange strip to make a 15 cm (6 in) strip. Commencing at the plain end, roll into a tight coil. Position this on the card and then add the eleven orange eyes (flower petals) radiating outwards from it. These should be squeezed almost flat. Add the stem. Position the leaves at the base of the stem. Glue everything to the card. Spread out the fringes of the flower centre.

HANGING LOBSTER CLAW
Heliconia rostrata

This pendent species of Heliconia is commonly called Lobster Claw, for obvious reasons! The brightly coloured, eye-catching bracts of this tropical plant, which last as cut flowers for up to twelve days, have made it one of the most popular and easily recognised tropical flowers in the world. Heliconias are members of the banana family, and this particular one hails from Colombia, Ecuador and Peru. It grows in clumps, in both full sun and semi-shade, to a height of 3 m (10 ft), and is an excellent greenhouse container plant in non-tropical climates.

Part	Quantity	Length	Shape	Colour
Trunk	21	5 cm (2 in)	triangle	dark green
Leaves	2	60 cm (24 in)	teardrop	dark green
Stems	21	5 cm ($^5/_8$ in)	strip	dark green
	1	15 cm (6 in)	strip	red
Bracts	9	10 cm (4 in)	teardrop	red
	8	15 cm (6 in)	leaf	yellow

To make the bracts, glue together a 10 cm (4 in) red teardrop and a 15 cm (6 in) yellow leaf. Make six 'buds' in this manner. You should have three red bracts remaining, and two yellow ones. Glue a yellow bract between two red ones, and glue the other yellow and red bracts on top, checking with the photo for placement. Then glue this 'flower' to one end of the red strip. Attach the 'bud' bracts to the stem, alternating them from one side to the other as illustrated.

Arrangement

Make the trunk by gluing the 5 cm (2 in) triangles one above the other for the full height of your card. Position the two leaves and their stems as desired and glue into place. Add the hanging stem of bracts, bending it into an attractive sinuous shape, so that the 'flower' bract overlaps the lower leaf slightly. Trim off any excess stem. My finished length was 10 cm (4 in).

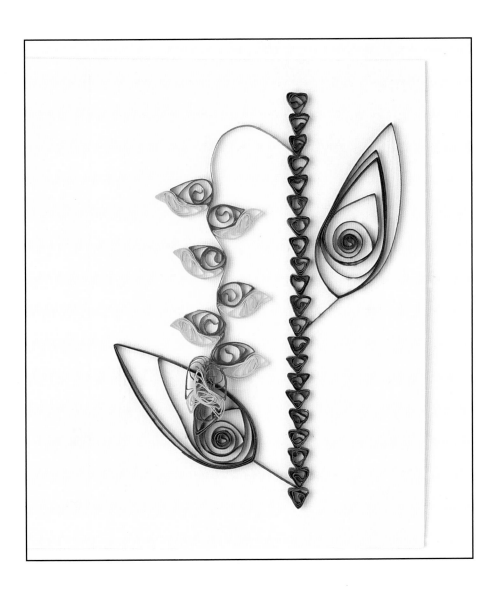

Quilling guilds

The following information on Quilling Guilds was kindly provided by the North American Quilling Guild and the Quilling Guild (UK) and is current as at the beginning of 2004. Every effort has been made to confirm that the details supplied are correct. The author was unable to find or confirm details of quilling guilds in other countries.

USA
North American Quilling Guild
PO Box 111, Cedar Grove,
NJ 07009-0111
http://www.naqg.org

CANADA
Joan Kiuru
1207–5959 Spring Garden Road
Halifax, Nova Scotia, B3H 1Y5
email: kiurujk@aol.com

UK
The Quilling Guild
Registration Officer
Shelia Harrop, 25 Littlefield Lane
Grimsby, Lincs. DN31 2LG
ENGLAND
email: sm.harrop25@ntlworld.com
http://www.quilling-guild.co.uk

THE NETHERLANDS
Dutch Filigraanvereneging
email: janetta_filigraan@xs4all.nl

ITALY
Mrs Barbara Mandrioli
Via Mascarelle 701/A
40224 Castel San Pietro Terme
Bologna
email: babla@supereva.it

SOUTH AFRICA
Mrs Diane Nineham
11 Gonubie Gardens,
Gonubie 5257
email: mwdi9ham@mweb.co.za

JAPAN

Mrs Shiro Ono
977-2 Ooka, Numazu
Shizuoka, 410-0022

AUSTRALIA

Mrs Meg Prance
49 Craig Street
Blacktown NSW 2148

Suppliers of quilling papers and equipment

The following list of suppliers of quilling equipment was compiled with assistance from the North American Quilling Guild and The Quilling Guild (UK) and is current as at the beginning of 2004. Every effort has been made by the author to confirm that the details supplied are correct.

Please note that this a only a small sample of suppliers and a search of your local telephone book will no doubt list a supplier closer to your home. The businesses listed are given as a guide only and are not necessarily endorsed by the author.

USA

Lake City Craft Company
1209 Eaglecrest Street
Box 2009, Nixa, MO 65714
Tel: (417)-725-8444
Fax: (417)-725-8448
http://www.quilling.com

National Artcraft
7996 Darrow Road
Twinsburg, OHIO 44087
Toll-free tel: 888-937-2723 (USA only)
Toll-free fax: 800-292-4916 (USA only)
Tel: 330-963-6011 (outside USA)
Fax: 330-963-6711 (outside USA)
email: sales@nationalartcraft.com
http://www.nationalartcraft.com

Whimsiquills
25 Indian Run
Enfield, CT 06082
Toll-free tel: 1-877-488-0894 (USA & Canada only)
Tel: (860) 749-0894
Fax: (860) 763-3904
http://www.whimsiquills.com

Quilled Creations
PO Box 492
Penfield, NY 14526
Tel. (585) 388-0706
email: sales@quilledcreations.com
http://www.quilledcreations.com/

Paplin's Products Inc.
435 Benefit Street
Pawtucket, RI 02861
Tel: 401-724-8558

Quill-It
PO Box 1304
Elmhurst, IL 60126

Maplewood Crafts
Humboldt Ind. Park
1 Maplewood Drive
Hazelton, PA 18201
Tel: 800-899-0134

Miz Bears Creations
2248 Obispo Avenue, Suite 206
Signal Hill, CA 90806
Tel: 562-498-7168

Christy Crafts
PO Box 491
Hinsdale, IL 60521
Tel: 630-323-6505

UK

Card Inspirations
The Old Dairy, Tewin Hill Farm
Tewin, Welwyn, Herts, AL6 0LL
Tel: +44 (0) 1438 717000
email: info@cardinspirations.co.uk
http://www.cardinspirations.co.uk

Craft Creations
Ingersoll House, Delamare Road
Cheshunt, Hertfordshire EN8 9HD
Tel: +44 (0) 1992 781900
Fax: +44 (0) 1992 634339
email enquiries@craftcreations.com
http://www.craftcreations.com

Crescent Quilling
4 High Street, Shoreham
Nr Sevenoaks, Kent TN14 7TD
Tel: +44 (0) 1959-525799
Fax: +44 (0) 1959-522513
e-mail: judy@CrescentQuilling.co.uk
http://www.crescentquilling.co.uk

J. J. Quilling Design
33 Mill Rise, Skidby, Cottingham
East Yorkshire HU16 5UA
Tel: +44 (0) 1482-843721
Fax: +44 (0) 1482 840783
email: enquiries@jjquilling.co.uk
http://www.janejenkins-
quillingdesign.co.uk

Crafty Quilling
91 Blackpool Road
Carleton near Blackpool,
Lancs FY6 7QH
Tel: +44 (0) 1253 884242
email: marjorie@craftyquilling.co.uk
http://www.craftyquilling.co.uk/

Evies Crafts

79 Dale Street, Milnrow

Rochdale, Lancashire, OL16 3NJ

Tel: +44 1706 712489

Craft Expressions

323 Upper Elmers End Road

Beckenham, Kent, BR3 3QP

Tel: +44 20 86589100

SOUTH AFRICA

Paper Flair

10 Umthi Close, Glenwood

Goodwood, 7460 Cape Town,

Western Province

Tel/Fax: +27 (0) 21 592 2480

http://capelink.co.za/home/paperflair/

Purple Hippo Creations

8 Stedman Mews

128 Jan Hofmeyr Rd, Westville 3630

PO Box 30132, Mayville 4058

Tel: +27 (0) 31 266 9416

Fax: +27 (0) 31 261 4380

email: mudpool@purplehippo.co.za

http://www.purplehippo.co.za/

PNA Strand

Shop 4, Die Dorpsmeent Centre

(opposite Post Office)

Main Road, Strand

PO Box 951, Strand 7139

Tel: +27 (0) 21-854 8108

Fax: +27 (0) 21-854 8121

email : info@pnastrand.co.za

http://www.pnastrand.co.za/

Spiral Crafts

Bettie or Ilsa

Tel: +27 (0) 82 335 7082

AUSTRALIA

Craft Lovers

Shop 1, 56 Murray Street, Tanunda,

South Australia

PO Box 474, Tanunda SA 5352

Tel: +61 8 8563 2370

Fax: +61 8 8563 0504

email: Craft.Lovers@portal.net.au

http://members.iweb.net.au/~craft/

Amelia's Crafts

50 Og Road, Klemzig, South Australia

PO Box 13, Klemzig SA 5087

Tel/Fax: +61 8 8369 2088

email: info@ameliascrafts.com.au

http://www.ameliascrafts.com.au/

Regal Craft Cards

24 Wellington St, Launceston

PO Box 7508, Launceston,

Tasmania 7250

Tel: +61 3 6331 4222

Fax: +61 3 6331 4904

email: info@regalcraftcards.com.au

http://www.regalcraftcards.com.au/

Stampcraft

Westralia Street Shopping Centre

9 Westralia Street, Stuart Park NT 0820

Tel: +61 (8) 8941 1066

Fax: +61 (8) 8941 1744

email: stampcraft@austarnet.com.au

http://www.stampcraft.com.au/index.html

Card Craft

Craft Corner, Stalls 406, 461 and 462

Paddy's Market, Haymarket, Sydney

PO Box 6015, Lake Munmorah

NSW 2259

Tel. +61 2 4358 1278

Fax. +61 2 4358 2167

email: cardcraft@quilling.com.au

http://www.quilling.com.au

Tranquil Pastimes

354B Chapel Road, Bankstown

PO Box 3530, Bankstown Square

NSW 2200

Tel: +61 (2) 9793 7774

Fax: +61 (2) 9708 0057

email: quilling@tranquilpastimes.com.au

http://www.tranquilpastimes.com.au

Novum Crafts

1761 Ferntree Gully Road

Ferntree Gully, Victoria 3156

Tel: +61 (3) 9758 3588

email: novum@novumcrafts.com.au

http://www.novumcrafts.com.au/

CANADA

Creative Paper Crafts

Angela's Craft Centre

37 King Street E., Dundas

Ontario L9H 1B7

Tel: 905-627-9905

Fax: 905-627-8704

Toll-free tel: 1-877-627-9905 (USA &

Canada only)

email:

customerservice@creativepapercrafts.com

http://www.angelascraftcentre.com

Canadian Craft Supplies

32 Major Street, Dartmouth

NS B2X 1A6

Fax: 902-435-9184

sales@canadiancraftsupplies.com

http://www.canadiancraftsupplies.com/

NEW ZEALAND

Daydreams

Larnoch Road, Henderson

(by appointment)

PO Box 69072, Glendene, Auckland

Tel: 09 837 0019

Fax: 09 837 0056

email: craftlover@daydreams.co.nz

http://www.daydreams.co.nz/

Hands Ashford New Zealand

5 Normans Road, Elmwood

Christchurch 5 New Zealand

Tel/Fax: 03 3559 099

email: hands.craft@clear.net.nz

http://www.hands.co.nz/